Deborah Heiligman

The Mysterious Ocean Highway

Benjamin Franklin and the Gulf Stream

A Division of Harcourt Brace & Company

www.steck-vaughn.com

For Phil Goldsmith,
another great Philadelphian

Steck-Vaughn Company

ISBN 0-7398-0013-2

For information about this and other Turnstone reference books and educational materials, visit Turnstone Publishing Group on the World Wide Web at http://www.turnstonepub.com.

Printed and bound in the United States of America

1 2 3 4 5 6 7 8 9 0 LB 04 03 02 01 00 99

Contents

1 The Mysterious Ocean Highway	4
2 Benjamin Franklin Maps the Gulf Stream	8
3 Studying the Gulf Stream	14
4 Cool Tools	26
5 The Wild Whirl of Water	36
Glossary	44
Further Reading	46
Index	47

1 The Mysterious Ocean Highway

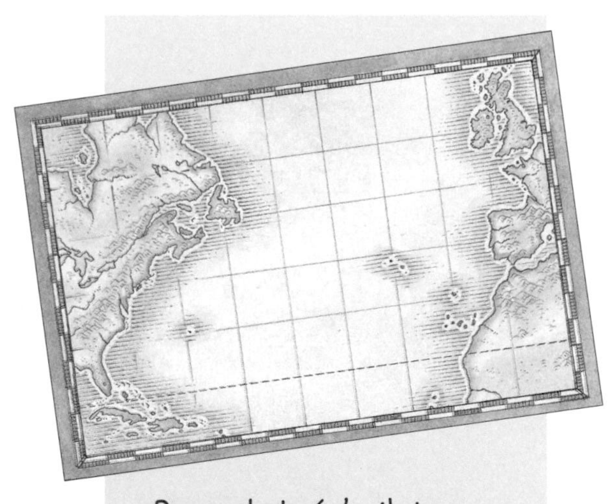

Ponce de León's pilot, Anton de Alaminos, understood the importance of the Gulf Stream. After de Alaminos established the path of the Gulf Stream, it became the routine path for Spanish ships traveling between North and South America and Spain.

In 1513 the Spanish explorer Juan Ponce de León set out to find the Fountain of Youth. Instead he found Florida—and a mysterious force in the ocean. His ships should have been sailing easily southward, the wind pushing them forward. But something was forcing them back.

What was pushing Ponce de León's ships back? Was it a giant sea creature? Was it magic? It wasn't a monster, and it wasn't magic. It was a very strong force in the ocean—a **current**. A current is a mass of moving water. A current can be a superhighway, pulling your ship along faster than the wind. However, if you get stuck in a current going the wrong way, watch out. It's like trying to go down an "up" escalator.

Ponce de León didn't realize what he had discovered. But his pilot, Anton de Alaminos, the person who was navigating the ships, knew they had found a powerful ocean current. He knew the current ran along the coast of North America and then turned toward Europe. The pilot thought that if they joined it, their ships could sail back to Spain faster than anyone else. He was right. Ponce de León and his crew had found the strongest current in the oceans—the Gulf Stream.

Sometimes sailors worked for the king or the queen of a country. The king or queen paid for the ships and the cost of each voyage. It was important to make trips as quickly as possible so that the ships could go out again to earn more money.

Over the years, other sailors also found the Gulf Stream, but they kept its path a secret. These sailors wanted to get their ships loaded with goods back to their king or queen or to the market faster than other sailors. So, much about the great current remained a mystery for centuries.

What Is the Gulf Stream?

What exactly is the Gulf Stream? Where does it go and why? Why is it so fast and strong? Winds help push currents along. However, that's not all that goes into making a powerful current like the Gulf Stream. For centuries sailors and scientists have tried to understand the "ocean superhighway."

Moving water though is very hard to keep track of and hard to study. An ocean is not a quiet pool of water, like a pond or a swimming pool, or even a lake. An ocean is a huge area of moving water. It has currents going across its surface and currents that run deep down, along the bottom of the ocean. There are also currents that move from top to bottom and from bottom to top. The ocean is a jumble of these different currents. The water in the ocean is also affected by what surrounds it—the coastline it runs past, the land underneath it, and the winds and weather above it.

All these things affect the Gulf Stream in different ways. When you look at it, the Gulf Stream current resembles a river in the ocean, but it

A **satellite** recording surface temperatures made this picture of our watery world. In it, the Gulf Stream looks turquoise. Many animals, such as seabirds, schools of fish, and turtles, live in and around the Gulf Stream.

Animals like this pilot whale often swim along the edges of the Gulf Stream where they find squid (their favorite food) and small fish to eat.

is not a simple line of moving water. A scientist named Rachel Carson, who studied and wrote about nature, called the Gulf Stream "narrow racing tongues of warm water that curl back in swirls and eddies." (An **eddy** is a current of water that moves in a different path from the rest of a current.) Uncovering the mysteries of the Gulf Stream's wild whirl of water has not been easy.

2 Benjamin Franklin Maps the Gulf Stream

Packets, like these ships in New York Harbor around 1830, sailed the same route over and over, carrying passengers, freight, and mail. The first packets to the Americas were British ships. After 1812 United States packets became more common, sailing up and down the East Coast.

The sailors who wanted to keep the Gulf Stream a secret didn't count on Benjamin Franklin. Benjamin Franklin was a great American **statesman**, an inventor, and a writer. He spent his life finding out how things worked, solving problems, and telling the world what he thought. When Franklin found out about the Gulf Stream, he wasn't about to keep it secret.

Franklin became interested in the Gulf Stream because of an everyday problem—slow mail. He was the Deputy Postmaster General of the American **colonies** from 1764 to 1775, and he was in charge of the mail for all the northern colonies. Franklin started a new mail system so that mail from Philadelphia to Boston took only three weeks instead of six. That made people happy, but there was still a problem with the mail coming from England.

Franklin learned that the mail ships making the two-month trip from England to the American colonies were taking two weeks longer than the merchant ships, which also came from England and carried goods for sale. How could that be? The mail ships, or "**packets**," as they were called, sailed from Falmouth, England, to New York. The merchant ships sailed from London, England, to Rhode Island. Some people wanted the mail ships to sail to Rhode Island instead of New York. They figured that would shorten the trip.

Franklin thought about it. From New York to Rhode Island was only a one-day trip by ship, so that wouldn't solve the problem. He thought about it some more. Merchant ships were heavier than mail ships, which would cause them to move more slowly. The merchant ships also had to travel down a river before leaving England, while the mail ships sailed right from the coast. The merchant ships should take longer. It was strange that they were taking two weeks less. He knew there must be something else going on.

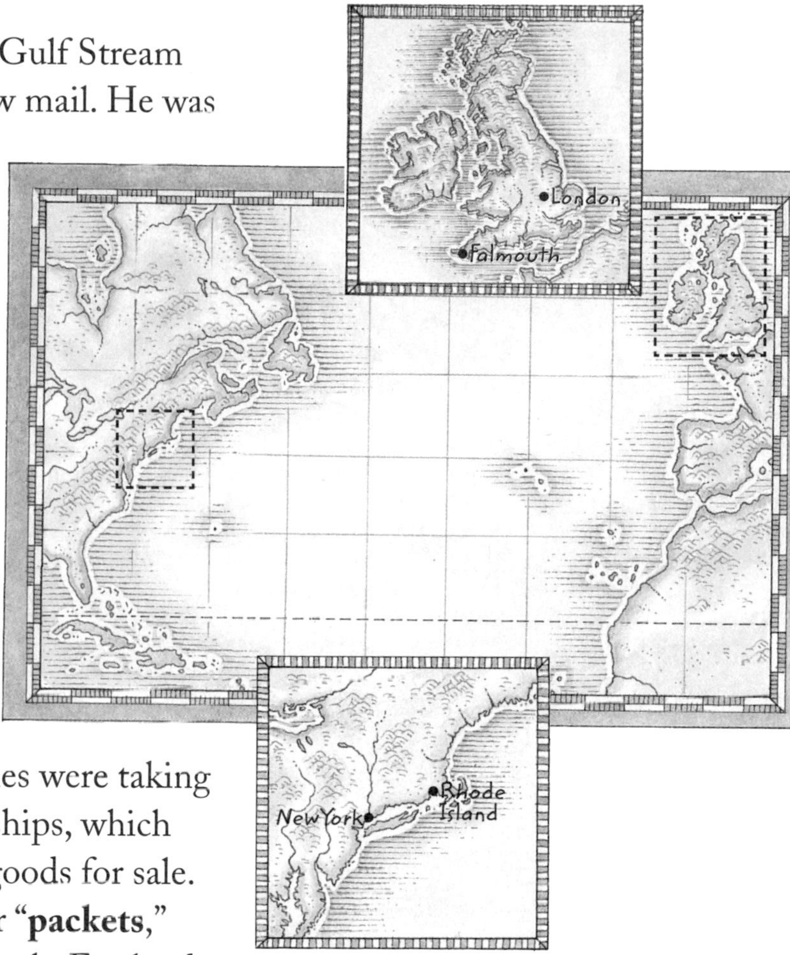

Packet ships bound for the American colonies sailed west from Falmouth, England. Merchant ships sailed from London.

Benjamin Franklin, Man of Many Talents

Benjamin Franklin (1706–1790) accomplished so much in his life that it's hard to say what makes him most famous. He was a statesman who encouraged trade with Native Americans and forged treaties with France and Great Britain. He was a printer, a newspaper and book publisher, and a writer. He made up sayings such as, "Early to bed and early to rise makes a man healthy, wealthy, and wise," "When the well's dry, we know the worth of water," and "Three may keep a secret if two of them are dead."

He was always looking for ways to improve the world around him. He started the country's first public library and helped start Philadelphia's first fire department. He argued against slavery.

Ben Franklin also invented an iron stove with a pipe that led outside. The stove kept houses warmer than a fireplace did. People still use Franklin stoves today. He also invented bifocal eyeglasses. Franklin didn't keep the rights to any of his inventions and gave away a lot of his money to charity.

Benjamin Franklin was also very curious. He was curious about Scottish tunes, sound, storms, comets, and how heat is absorbed by different colors. He experimented with electricity by flying a kite in a thunderstorm. He proved that electricity and lightning are the same thing.

Franklin spent a lot of time on ships, and he had many different ideas about ways to make sailing safer. One of his inventions was a sea **anchor** (left). This was an anchor that had a cloth behind it that worked like a parachute. The anchor kept the parachute under the water's surface, and the pull of the water against the parachute slowed down the ship. Franklin thought the sea anchor would be useful in a storm, when the wind might push a ship onto the shore or into a reef. He was right, and almost every ship now carries a type of sea anchor.

Franklin Charts the Gulf Stream

Franklin was a smart person, but he didn't have all the answers. Like any good scientist or researcher, he knew that often the best way to find the answer to a question is to ask somebody else who might know. That's just what he did.

Franklin was in London while he was trying to solve this problem of speeding mail delivery from England. It happened that his cousin, Timothy Folger, was in London, too. Folger was the captain of a whaling ship. Franklin thought that his cousin might be able to help him figure out the riddle of the two-week difference. Folger said that was easy—the merchant ship captains knew about the Gulf Stream and how to avoid it on the trip back to the colonies. The packet captains didn't.

Folger knew about the Gulf Stream. So did all the whaling captains. They knew where the Stream was because whales often swam at its edges eating the squid and fish there. Captains knew the Stream ran along the coast of North America going north, and then turned eastward in the North Atlantic toward Europe. Sailing toward Europe, it was great to join the current. It got ships there faster. But coming back from Europe, the Stream moved in the wrong direction. If ships going westward got caught in the current, it slowed them down. The whaling captains knew to avoid the Gulf Stream going from Europe to the Americas.

Folger told Franklin that whaling captains often crossed the Gulf Stream to get to the whales on the other side. Sometimes they met mail packets in the middle of the Gulf Stream, sailing against the current. The whaling captains told the packet captains to get out of the current that

(above)
Timothy Folger was a whaling captain and merchant in Nantucket, Massachusetts, a whaling center in the mid 1700s.

(below)
In the 1700s and 1800s, most whaling was done from ships like this New England whaling ship.

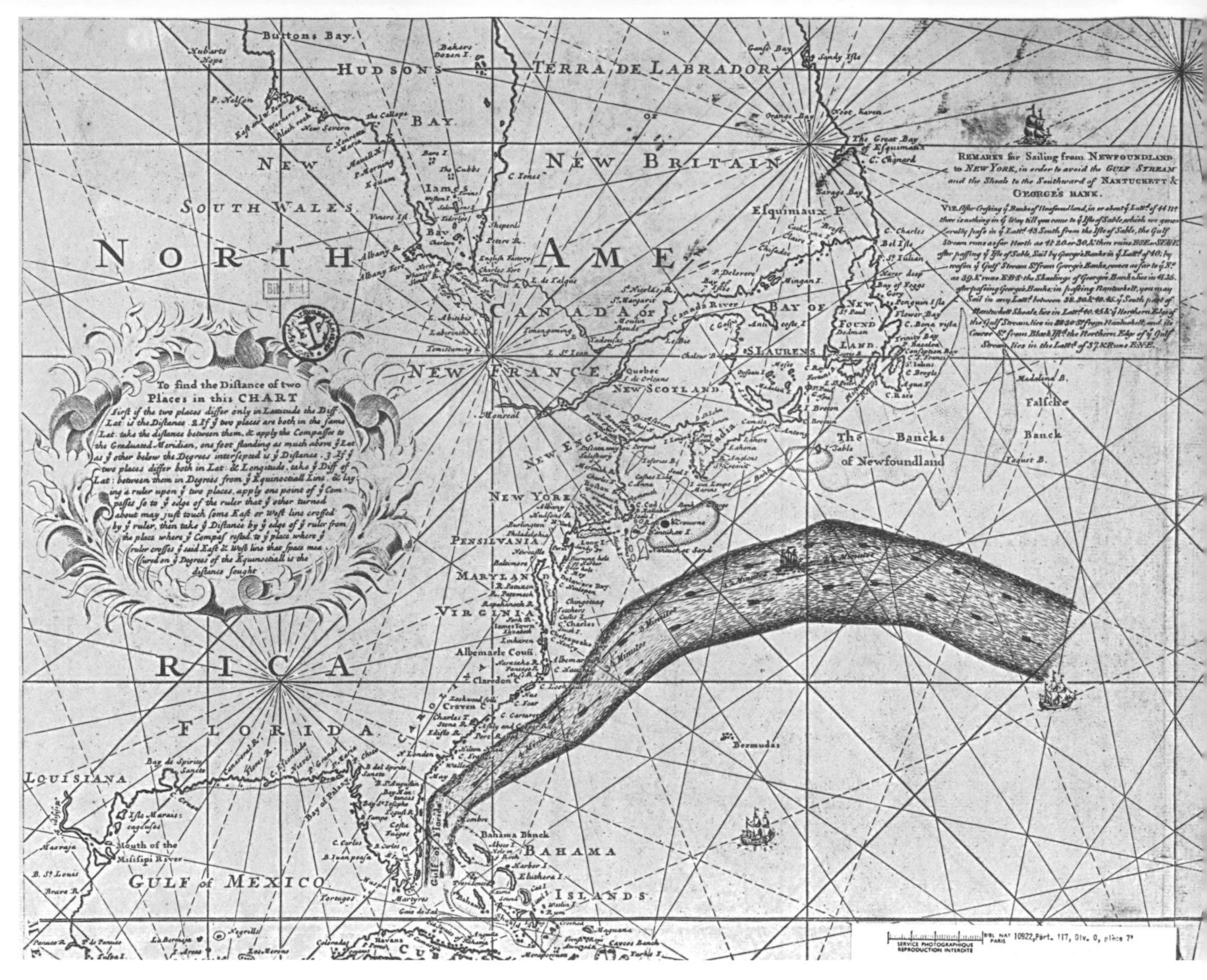

This Franklin-Folger chart, first published around 1769, was made using information from whalers and other sailors. It included notes about how to avoid shoals, or shallow water, and the warning that if a ship strayed into the Gulf Stream, it would be slowed by 60 to 70 miles a day.

was slowing them down "to the value of three miles an hour." "But," Folger told his cousin, "they were too wise to be counseled by simple American fishermen."

The merchant ships, like the whalers, knew enough not to become caught in that powerful current. That's why they were making the trip faster.

Franklin asked Folger to sketch the path of the Gulf Stream on a **chart**. Ocean charts are maps that show coastlines, water depth, and other information. Folger did, and he also wrote directions so that ships could avoid the Gulf Stream when sailing from Europe to North America.

What Folger drew looked like a river in the ocean, a band of water moving from the east coast of the American colonies north and east toward

England and the rest of Europe. Franklin could see that if a ship got caught in the Gulf Stream coming back from England, that current would be moving against it.

Franklin knew right away that the packet captains needed a chart that showed the path of the Gulf Stream. Between 1769 and 1770, he had copies printed in London, with his cousin's sailing advice written on the chart.

The Franklin-Folger chart was the first chart of the Gulf Stream. So add cartographer, or mapmaker, to the list of Benjamin Franklin's accomplishments.

Franklin's Chart is Lost

But the British mail ships ignored the chart. Why? Franklin had used a map that was about a hundred years old to show the Gulf Stream. So other than the Gulf Stream path, Franklin's chart was out of date. Is that why the packet captains didn't use it? Perhaps. But it was probably just that they didn't want to take advice from Americans, the same way they didn't want to listen to the whaling captains. In any case, they ignored it. Even though Franklin tried to help, it still took two weeks longer than it had to for the colonists to get their mail.

Not long after that, in 1776, the American colonies declared their independence from the British, and the Revolutionary War began. British ships were now sailing to America for a totally different reason—to fight the colonists. That chart of the Gulf Stream might have been helpful to the British Navy, but it seems they never saw it.

Since the packet captains lost the map, they probably never showed it to the British Navy. The packets might have even thrown the maps away. Or perhaps there were so few copies that they just got lost. No one knows for sure. But what is certain is that the chart disappeared. It was lost for nearly two hundred years.

3 Studying the Gulf Stream

In Franklin's time, the best tool for measuring ocean temperatures was the Cavendish thermometer (below). The thermometer could survive in the sea and in rough weather, but it wasn't reliable at deep water depths.

The thermometer was made of glass. The height of the mercury indicated the temperature.

The light part of the thermometer was filled with alcohol.

The dark parts of the thermometer were filled with mercury.

Franklin became so curious about the Gulf Stream after charting it that he became one of the first people to study it. During his career as an agent for the colonies in London, Franklin sailed back and forth across the Atlantic Ocean many times. Even when he was was old and often in pain from an illness called gout, he just couldn't resist the chance to experiment. He lowered a **thermometer** over the side of the ship to measure the temperature of the water. When his ship left the Gulf Stream, he measured the temperature of the sea again. By comparing the temperatures, Ben Franklin showed that the Gulf Stream water is warmer than the water on either side of it.

In 1776 Franklin went on a hurried secret mission to France to ask for their help in the war. He took his grandsons Temple, almost seventeen, and Benjamin Franklin Bache, seven, with him. Although he had a lot on his mind, he measured water temperatures, this time with his grandsons' help. After he arrived in France, he had another Gulf Stream chart printed.

In 1785, having spent many years in Europe, Franklin sailed back to what was now the United States of America. It was Franklin's last trip across the Atlantic.

Here is a record of temperature readings Franklin made during a 1775 trip on the packet *Pennsylvania*, which sailed from London to Philadelphia.

Franklin first wrote down the reading date.

The reading time was added if there was more than one reading that day.

Date		Hour.	Temp. of Air.	Temp. of Wat.	Latitude N.		Longitude W.	
April	10			62				
	11			61				
	12			64				
	13			65				
	14			65	°	'	°	'
	26		60	70	37	39	60	38
	27		60	70	37	13	62	29
	28	8A.M.	70	64	37	48	64	35
	—	6 P.M.	67	60				
	29	8A.M.	63	71	37	26	66	0
	—	5 P.M.	65	72				
	—	11 dit.	66	66				
	30	8A.M.	64	70				
	—	12	62	70	37	20	68	53
	—	6 P.M.	64	72				
	—	10 dit.	65	65				
May	1	7A.M.	68	63				
	—	12	65	56	38	13	72	23
	—	4 P.M.	64	56				
	—	10 dit.	64	57				
	2	8A.M.	62	53	38	43	74	3
	—	12	60	53				
	—	6 P.M.	64	55				
	—	10 dit.	65	55				
	3	7 A.M.	62	54	38	30	75	0

Warmer water temperature meant the ship was in Gulf Stream waters.

Franklin used measurements called latitude and longitude to note where the ship was at each reading. This helped him locate the Gulf Stream.

Recording both air and water temperatures could show they were linked.

Latitude and Longitude

If you look at a globe, you'll see lines running sideways around it. These lines are called *parallels*. The up-and-down, or vertical, lines are called *meridians*. Sailors find their locations using these parallels and meridians. The parallel that divides north from south on the globe is called the **equator**. The meridian that divides east from west on the globe is called the *prime meridian*. The equator and the prime meridian are the starting points for measuring **latitude** and **longitude**.

Parallels measure latitude, the distance north or south from the equator. Meridians measure longitude, the distance east or west from the prime meridian.

Both latitude and longitude are measured in degrees. The equator is 0° degrees latitude and the prime meridian is 0° longitude. For example, New Orleans, Louisiana, is 30° N latitude and 90° W longitude.

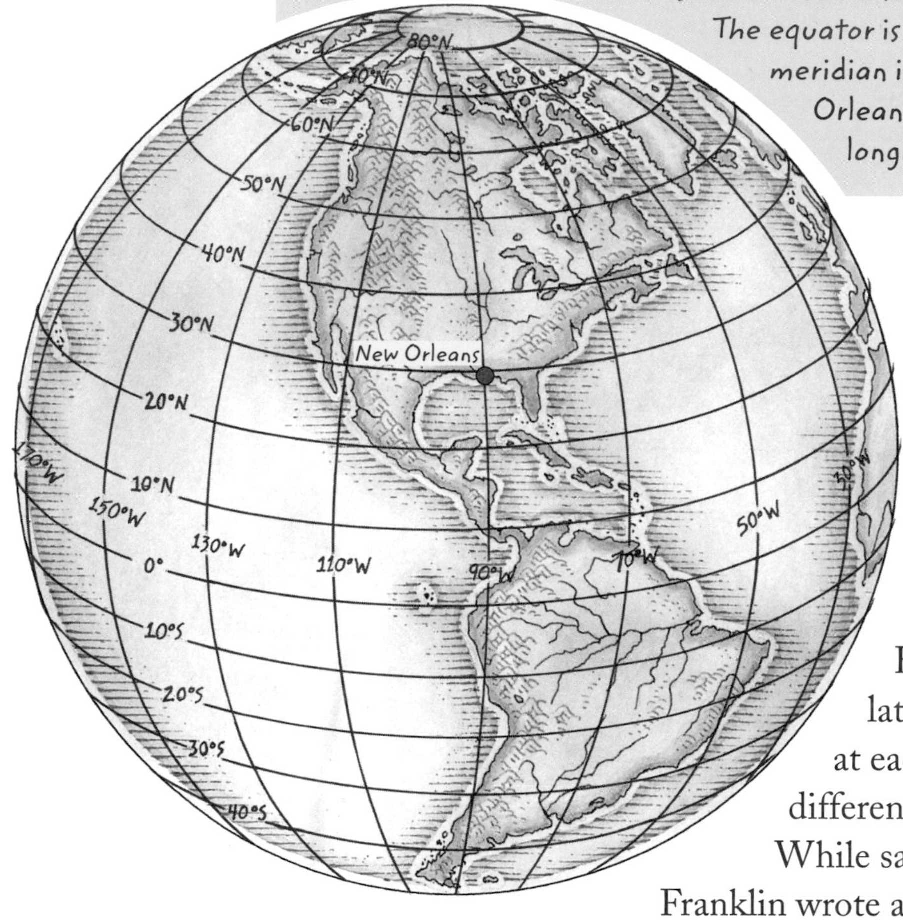

This time Franklin brought his grandnephew Jonathan Williams, Jr., to help him study the Gulf Stream. Franklin was now 79 years old. On this trip he wanted to measure the temperature of the water not just on the surface, but as far down as a hundred feet. He did it at first with a bottle and later with a barrel fitted with a valve at each end. He also took notes on the different colors of the water that they saw.

While sailing back to the colonies in 1785, Franklin wrote about his research at sea in a paper called "Maritime Observations." In it he describes making the first chart with his cousin. Once back in Philadelphia he published that paper. A third version of the Gulf Stream chart was included with the paper. It wasn't as accurate as the first or second charts, but it included some of the research he had done with his grandsons and grandnephew. Add **oceanographer** to his list of accomplishments.

After Ben Franklin died in 1790, his grand-nephew Jonathan Williams, Jr., continued to take measurements of the water. A few years later, Williams found an eddy of warm water from the Gulf Stream moving in a circle. Today scientists continue to study eddies, or **rings**, like the one Williams found.

Except for Williams, it was almost one hundred years after Franklin's first Gulf Stream chart was made that people began to study the Gulf Stream seriously. One of these people, Alexander Bache, was a great-grandson of Benjamin Franklin. Another was Lieutenant Matthew Maury.

Bache and Maury did not work together. In fact, they were rivals, which means they competed against each other. Each thought the Gulf Stream was his to study—and his alone. Bache was the **superintendent** of the U.S. Coast Survey, and he thought the Gulf Stream was his to study because it touched the coast of the United States. Maury was a lieutenant in the U.S. Navy, and he thought the Gulf Stream was his to study because it was part of the oceans. Of course, nobody can "own" a current in the ocean. But the **rivalry** between Bache and Maury was good for science, as rivalry sometimes is. Working to outdo each other, each added greatly to our understanding of the Gulf Stream.

Alexander Bache was not only Benjamin Franklin's great-grandson but also a college professor and the first president of the National Academy of Sciences.

Bache Studies the Stream

As the superintendent of the U.S. Coast Survey, Bache was the first person to study the Gulf Stream using a system. He ordered ships to cross the Gulf Stream over a dozen times. Sailors measured the temperature of the water at many different depths at various places in the Gulf Stream. They recorded all their positions using latitude and longitude,

(above)
Matthew Maury had been a sea captain, but he was so badly hurt in a stagecoach accident that he had to retire from the sea.

(below)
Maury received pages from logbooks of whaling ships, like these pages from the logbook of the ship *Black Sea* during a voyage from Hampton Roads, Virginia, to New South Wales, Australia, in 1857.

imaginary lines around the globe that sailors use to describe a location, each time they made a measurement. Bache then put all the **data** together to make a picture of the Gulf Stream. His brother, Lieutenant George Bache, who was at sea, helped him, too.

The Bache brothers discovered that bands of water with different temperatures run through the Gulf Stream. Alexander Bache also found evidence that there was a current running under the Gulf Stream in the opposite direction. The technology didn't exist yet to prove the deeper current was really there. But years later another scientist working on the Gulf Stream would prove that Alexander Bache was right.

Maury's Treasure

While the Bache brothers were measuring features of the Gulf Stream by ship, Maury was studying it from a dusty old storeroom. He was the head of the Navy's Depot of Charts and Instruments. When he started his new job, he discovered that the

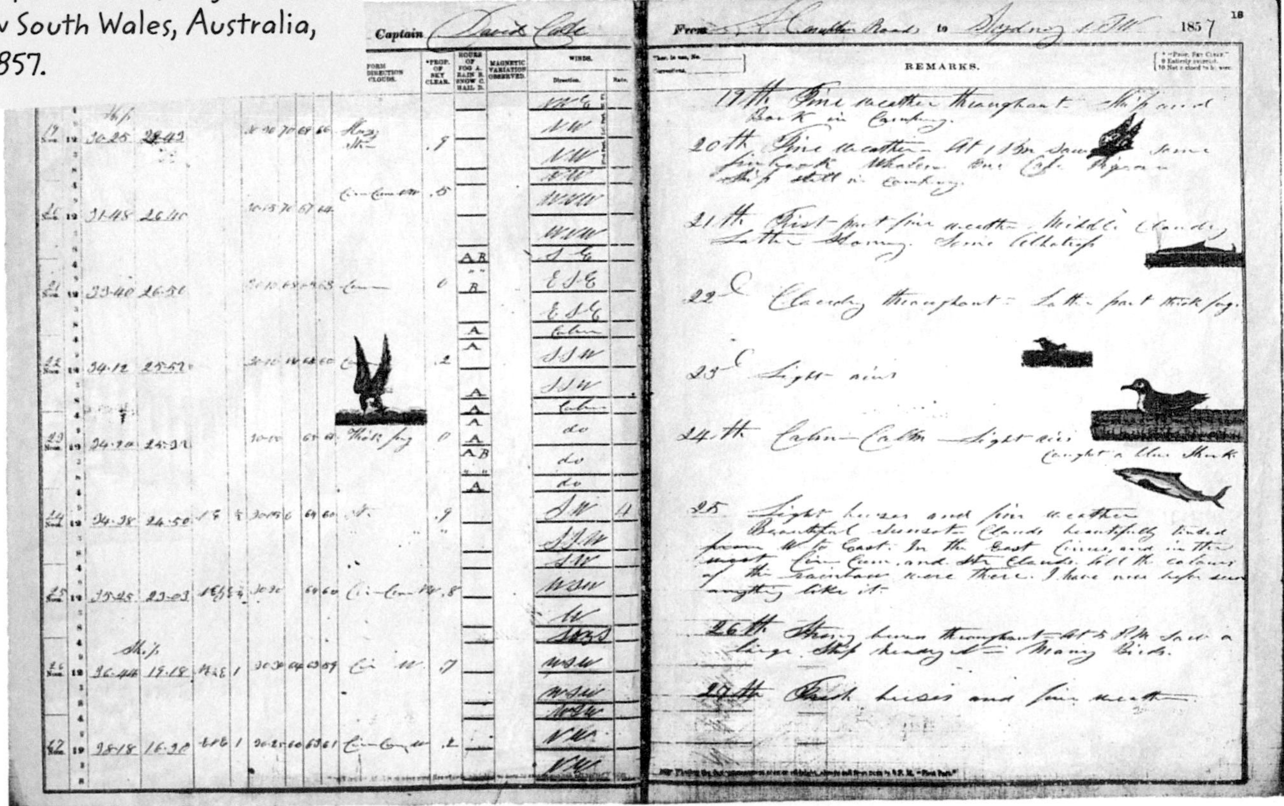

Captain

From Hampton Roads to Sydney N.S.W. 1857

REMARKS.

19th Fine weather throughout. Ship and Bark in Company.
20th Fine weather. At 11 am saw some finback Whales. One Cape Pigeon. Ship still in Company.
21th First part fine weather. Middle Cloudy. Latter Stormy. Some Albatross
22d Cloudy throughout. Latter part thick fog.
23d Light airs
24th Calm—Calm—Light airs. Caught a blue Shark
25 Light breezes and fine weather. Beautiful sunset. Clouds beautifully tinted from W to East. In the East Cirrus, and in the West Cirr Cum. and Str Clouds. All the colours of the Rainbow were there. I have never before seen anything like it.
26th Strong breezes throughout. At 5 PM saw a large Ship heading N— Many Birds.
27th Fresh breezes and fine weather

Navy had very few ocean charts. He searched through the Depot's storeroom and found what he knew was a treasure—logbooks from Navy ships.

A ship's logbook holds records of each trip the ship makes. Every day the captain writes down the ship's location. The captain also records the speed of currents and winds and describes the weather and anything else important that has happened on the ship that day.

Maury sorted the logbooks into piles by where each ship went. He put logbooks of ships sailing from New York to London in one pile and logbooks of ships sailing from Boston to Florida in another pile, and so on. Then, he looked at the books in each pile. He studied them to get an idea of where ocean currents and winds were. It was slow work, but he started to see patterns. He was able to plot, or draw, currents and winds on the ocean charts, just as Franklin and his cousin had plotted the Gulf Stream from the whaling captains' experiences. But Maury needed more logbooks. He asked sea captains from merchant ships to make records and send them to him. That was a lot of work, and not very many did it. Still, in 1847, Maury published a series of charts called Wind and Current Charts.

At first, most captains ignored the charts—just as British captains had ignored Franklin's Gulf Stream chart. But a few captains tried using them and made much better time. Franklin had said, "Remember that time is money." The faster a ship could make a trip, the sooner it could go back out and make more money. Soon everybody wanted the charts, but Maury said they were not for sale. The only way a ship's captain could get a chart was to send in a logbook so that Maury could get more information. Soon Maury had a thousand volunteers.

Bache and Maury used the Six thermometer, shown below, invented in 1794 by James Six. It could record high and low temperatures. It was more reliable than the Cavendish thermometer (see page 14), but still didn't work well in the deep ocean.

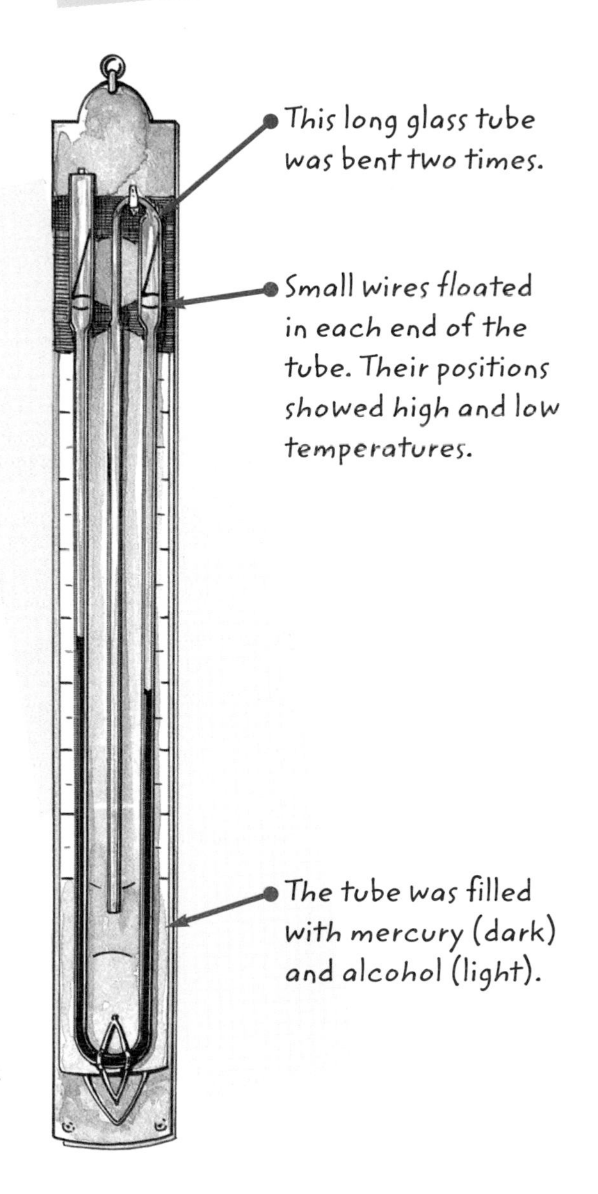

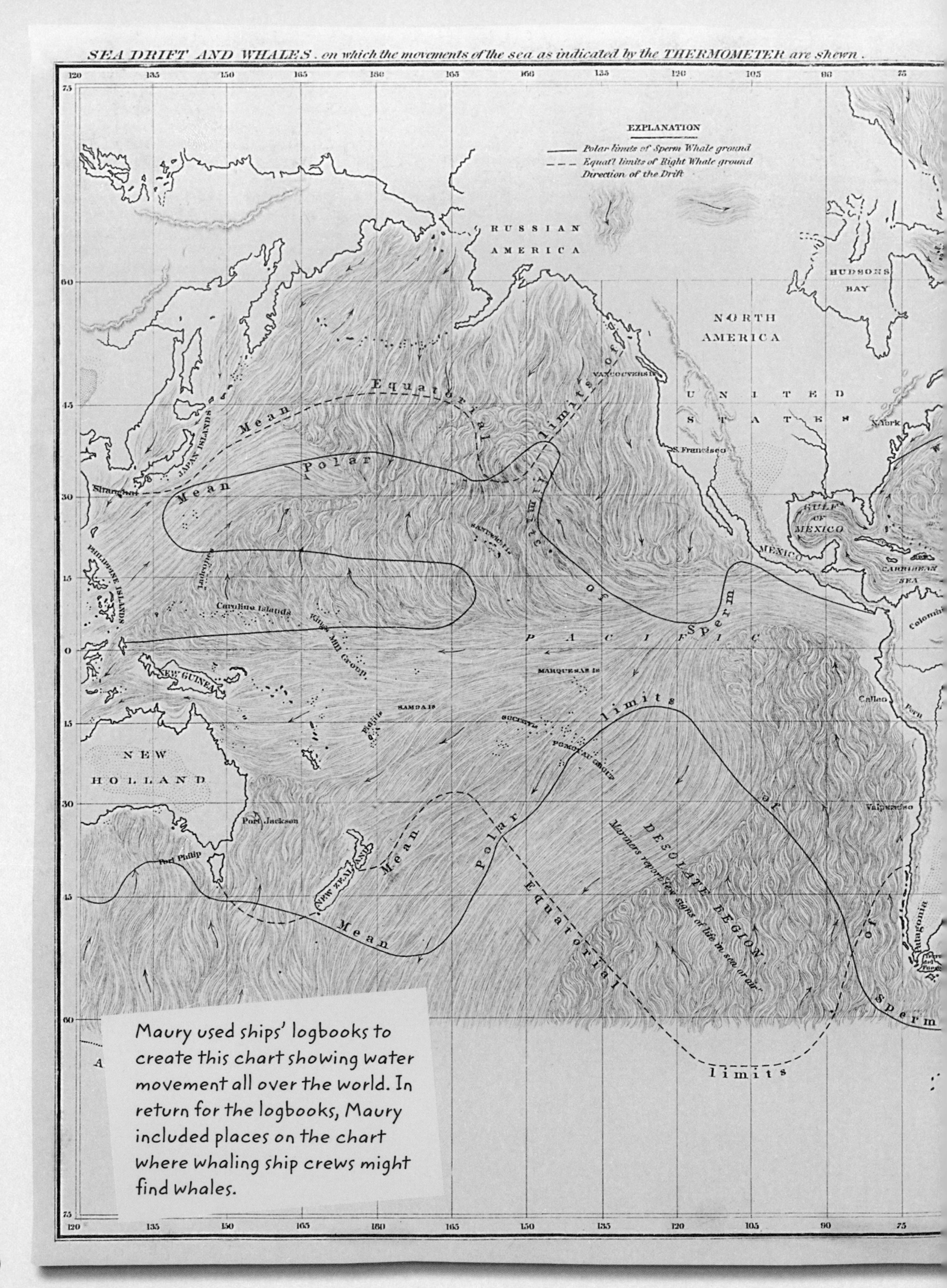

Maury used ships' logbooks to create this chart showing water movement all over the world. In return for the logbooks, Maury included places on the chart where whaling ship crews might find whales.

Plate XIV
GREENLAND
Iceland
NORWAY
SWEDEN
North Sea
Baltic Sea
RUSSIA
ASIA
EUROPE
Inland Basin
France
Spain
Portugal
ITALY
TURKEY
Black Sea
Caspian Sea
MEDITERRANEAN
Algeria
Madeira
Canary Is.
Morocco
Tripoli
Barca
PERSIA
ARABIA
CHINA
Canton
Sargasso Sea
AFRICA
ARABIAN SEA
Bombay
Calcutta
HINDOSTAN
BAY OF BENGAL
COCHIN CHINA
C. d. Verde Is.
Senegambia
Guinea
Abyssinia
Gulf of Guinea
ATLANTIC
BORNEO
SUMATRA
INDIAN OCEAN
MOZAMBIQUE
MADAGASCAR
St. Helena
Rio de Janeiro
Right whale ground
whale ground
Cape Town
Georgia
Sandwich Land
Icy barrier

Maury to the Rescue

Maury proved how valuable his research was by saving a ship in distress. The ship *San Francisco*, damaged in a storm, was drifting helplessly in the middle of the Atlantic Ocean. Using his current charts, Maury predicted where the ship would drift. He made an "X" where he thought the ship would be by the time rescuers could arrive. The rescuers set out and found the ship at almost the exact spot Maury had marked.

After Maury's death, the U.S. Navy began to publish charts of the North Atlantic showing where abandoned ships were floating. These ships, called derelicts, had been damaged at sea and left drifting. Being wooden, the ships didn't sink, so they could be dangerous to other ships. Many derelicts, like USS *Granite State* shown here, stayed afloat for six months or longer.

Continuing Maury's tradition, the derelict charts were free to navigators in return for their reports of weather, winds, and currents.

Maury also came up with another way to study the movement of currents—putting messages in bottles. A few times during a trip, a sailor would write down the ship's location, put it in a bottle, and throw the bottle overboard. The bottles were swept away by currents and finally landed on beaches along the Atlantic Ocean. Inside each bottle was a message asking the finder to send the information inside the bottle to Maury along with a note telling where the bottle was found. Using this method, Maury learned where the bottle was dropped off the ship and where it had drifted. With enough bottle messages, Maury was able to determine where currents were and to add them to his charts.

As Maury worked, the path and the strength of the Gulf Stream became clearer and clearer. "There

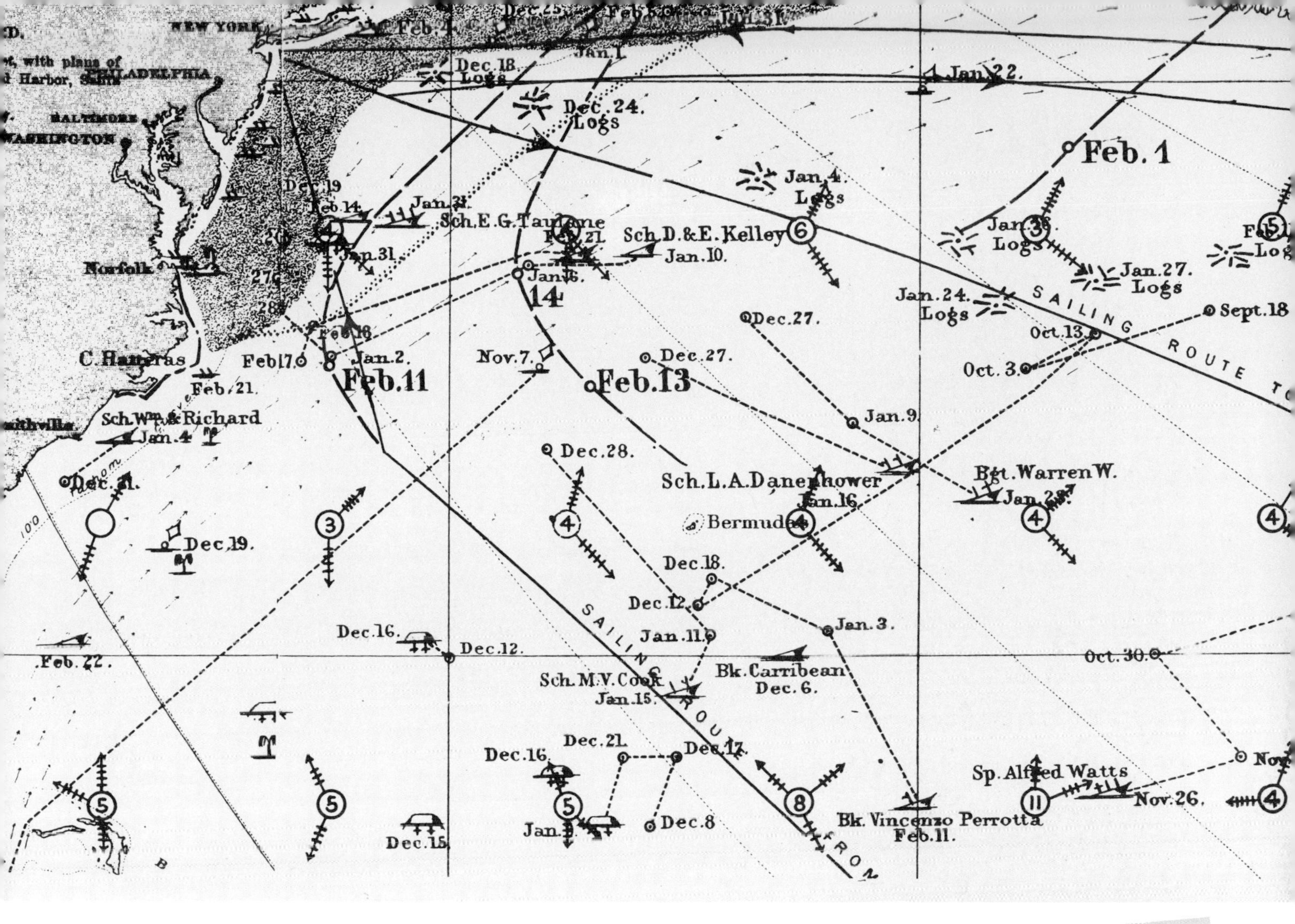

is a river in the ocean," he wrote. "Its banks and bottom are of cold water, while its current is of warm. . . . It is the Gulf Stream."

As time went on, however, people began to suspect that the Gulf Stream was more than a river in the ocean. Toward the end of the nincteenth century, after Maury and Bache had died, people began to wonder where the Gulf Stream ended. No one knew for sure. Some people said it ended in the eastern Atlantic. Others said the Stream split, with some of it going north past Great Britain and the rest moving south down the coast of Europe. It's not always a trained scientist who finds the answer to an important question. In this case, it was a prince who figured out what happens to the Gulf Stream after it leaves the coast of the United States.

This 1888 chart shows the locations and dates of derelict ship sightings. The drawings of ships show whether the ship seen was floating right-side up or upside down. Derelict ships floated with the ocean currents. The paths of the ships are shown by dashed lines. Taken all together, the paths of these ships traced the paths of the Gulf Stream. Other symbols on the chart show drifting **buoys**, steamship paths, and other information useful for sailors.

(above)
Prince Albert of Monaco used the Negretti and Zambra thermometer to study the Gulf Stream.

(below right)
The Negretti and Zambra thermometer was basically a Six thermometer (see page 19) with extra protection so that it could record temperatures in deeper or colder water.

Message in a Bottle

Prince Albert (1848–1922) was the prince of Monaco, a tiny country on the southeast coast of France. He spent a lot of time sailing and became very curious about the Gulf Stream. He decided to do some of his own investigating. He dropped glass bottles, copper balls, and wooden barrels into the Gulf Stream. Inside each object was a request in ten languages to send a note to Prince Albert telling where and when the object was found. By studying the notes, the prince learned that the Gulf Stream splits in the northeastern Atlantic Ocean. Part of the stream heads toward Ireland and Great Britain

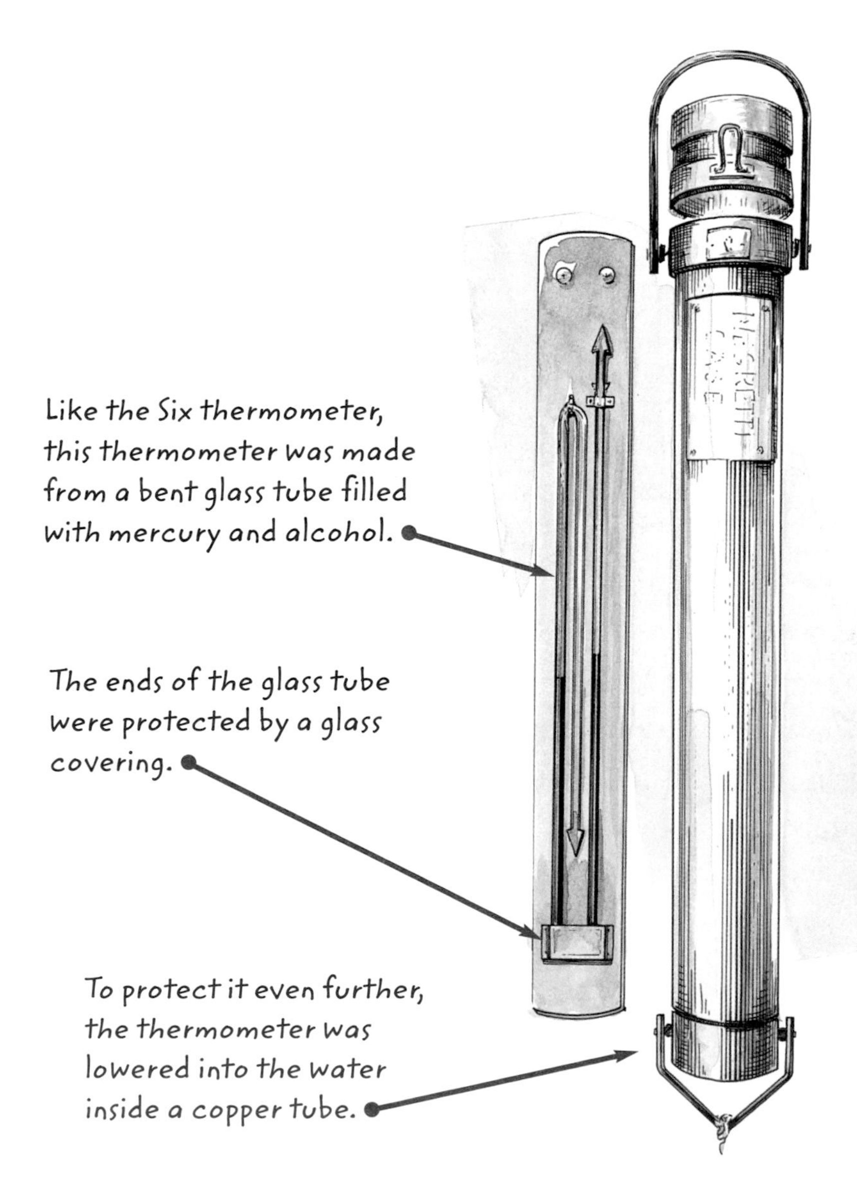

and then mixes with the rest of the water in the North Atlantic. The second part of the Gulf Stream heads south past Spain and Africa, and then turns west.

Prince Albert's studies helped scientists begin to understand that the Gulf Stream is not just one current. It is part of a larger system of currents in the North Atlantic Ocean. The prince's studies also helped save lives. At the end of World War I, using what he knew about currents, Prince Albert was able to predict the direction that drifting mines, which were a kind of wartime explosive device, would take. At least sixty mines were found on beaches on both sides of the Atlantic. They had drifted just the way Prince Albert said they would. Experts were able to disarm the mines before they exploded.

Over the years, Prince Albert dropped more than 1,500 bottles and barrels with messages inside into the Gulf Stream and studied the results in his laboratory.

4 Cool Tools

A ship's crew launches a tool called a CTD. It measures the saltiness and temperature of ocean water at different depths.

In the past sailors and scientists studied the Gulf Stream mainly to know where it was. They wanted to know the path of the Stream so that ships could use it to move more quickly and safely. Whalers wanted to know its path so they could find pods of whales that fed on animals at the edges of the Gulf Stream.

Today scientists around the world study the Gulf Stream for different reasons. Scientists want to find out exactly how the Stream affects temperatures in the ocean and on Earth. They also want to find out how changes on Earth, such as colder or warmer temperatures, might affect the Stream's temperature and its path, and if changes in the Stream could mean changes for the animals that depend on the Stream.

To find out, oceanographers study the Stream at different places, recording its temperature, how fast it moves, where it moves, how salty it is, and what plants and animals can be found in it. By looking at all this information, scientists can better understand how the Gulf Stream changes and is changed by everything around it.

To help them study the Gulf Stream, scientists have invented new tools and improved old tools that were used by Benjamin Franklin, Matthew Maury, and Prince Albert.

Modern oceanographic thermometers, like the XBT shown below, take measurements of ocean temperatures at many different depths. Some XBTs can send their measurements up to satellites, so scientists don't even have to be on a ship to get the information they need.

The XBT is connected to the ship by wire that spools out from the top.

Temperature is recorded by a device called a thermistor. It takes temperature readings as the XBT moves through the water.

Information from the thermistor is relayed to the ship through the wire in the lower spool, which also spools out.

A scientist launches an XBT.

Drifter buoys like this Global Lagrangian Drifter carry several instruments at once. The drifters are released into the ocean from planes or launched from ships. The instruments measure the speed and direction of water near the surface.

Benjamin Franklin was one of the first people to use a thermometer to understand the paths of ocean currents. Today scientists who study the temperature of the Gulf Stream still use thermometers. But while Franklin's thermometer could only take readings from one location at a time, today's thermometers are able to record different temperature readings as the ship moves. These temperatures are then charted on a graph. The graphs help scientists see how the Stream's temperature changes from place to place and get a more accurate picture of where the current is.

A barometer and sunlight gauge are on top of the surface float.

The buoy that floats at the surface has a built-in antenna to send information up to satellites. It also has sensors to measure water temperature.

The material of the "holey sock" fabric tube drags through the water, pulling on the buoy. This keeps the buoy from moving with the wind instead of with the ocean currents.

Weights help keep the buoy stable, upright, and moving with the current.

Floating Objects Show the Gulf Stream's Path

Matthew Maury and Prince Albert of Monaco both studied the Gulf Stream by keeping track of the movement of objects, like bottles, that floated or drifted with the current. Scientists today still use floating objects to study the Gulf Stream. These devices are called drifters, **floats**, and buoys. Some of these objects are able to send signals to satellites high overhead, which then report the objects' movements to scientists.

One of these devices, called a Swallow float, was able to prove that a hundred-year-old hypothesis, or educated guess, was true. In the 1950s, Henry Stommel, a scientist at Woods Hole Oceanographic Institution (or WHOI, pronounced "HOO-ee") located in Woods Hole, Massachusetts, began to wonder how deeply the Gulf Stream flowed and what path it took as it moved underwater. He heard that a person named John Swallow had designed a float to study currents that run under the ocean's surface.

A modern-day Swallow float is launched. The glass balls on top of the float hold batteries and electronic equipment and help keep the float from sinking. The aluminum tube makes a sound signal that can be heard at a receiving station. When the float reaches a certain depth, it starts to drift and measure the current at that depth.

Stommel knew just how he wanted to use Swallow floats. Like Alexander Bache almost a hundred years earlier, Stommel believed that there was a deep ocean current running in the opposite direction of the Gulf Stream. He convinced himself this was so by doing a very complicated math problem. But Stommel needed a way to prove to others that he was right. So he and Swallow dropped Swallow floats into the Gulf Stream. By using these floats, they were able to prove that there was a deep current under the Gulf Stream. It became known as the Deep Water Western Boundary Current.

RAFOS floats run on C and D batteries—lots of them. When a RAFOS float's batteries run out, it is left in the ocean. Oceanographers say that it is just too expensive to retrieve each float. Some floats wash ashore or are picked up by fishers. Most continue to float for a time, and seaweed often grows on them. They are not dangerous to ocean animals.

Today, Amy Bower, an oceanographer at WHOI, uses a new kind of float to study the Deep Western Boundary Current. It is called a RAFOS float. A RAFOS float is small and made of glass. It drifts with the current and records signals from sound **transmitters** attached to the ocean bottom. When Amy reads the signals the floats pick up, she can tell where the floats have been and track the path of the current that carried them along.

Amy has given RAFOS floats to crews on ships that make the same trips over and over, such as passenger ships, freighters, and oil tankers. A RAFOS float weighs only 10 kilograms (about 22 pounds) and can easily be dropped over the side of a boat by one person. Each float is usually set to work for a year or longer. When that time is up, the glass tube pops to the surface, sends the data to a satellite, and the satellite sends the data to a station on the ground. The data then go to Amy's computer.

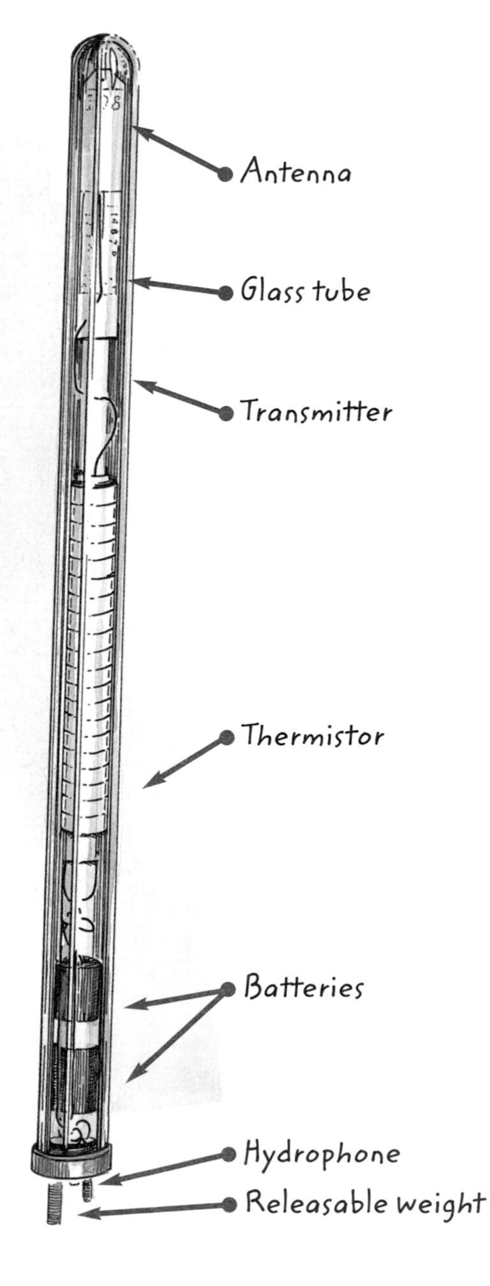

Unlike earlier floats, which were large and very heavy, RAFOS floats are portable. "Anyone can put a RAFOS float in the water," says researcher Amy Bower.

An oceanographer is testing a current meter in a lab before sending it out to sea.

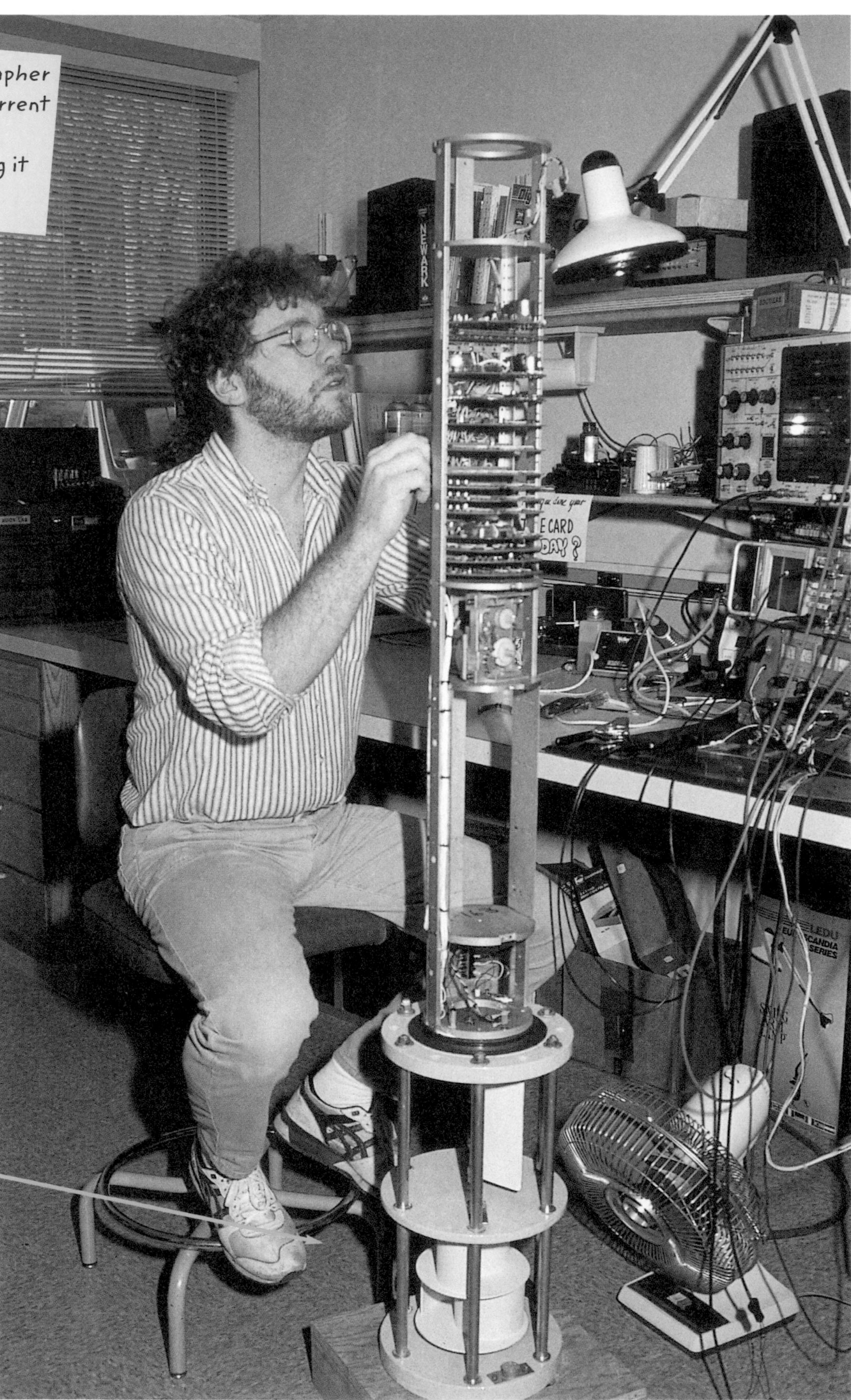

The wheel at the bottom spins to measure the speed of the current. This meter is being tested. A fan blows air onto the wheel to make it spin.

Tools Old and New

Oceanographers are interested not only in where the current goes, but also in how fast it moves and how much it varies. In Franklin's time whaling captains figured out the speed of the Gulf Stream by seeing how fast a small boat in the Stream moved away from the whaling ship. Today current meters measure the speed of the water. A current meter is a device that's attached to a wire rope and an anchor. This keeps the meter in one place while the water rushes by it, causing a little wheel on the meter to spin. The faster the current, the faster the wheel spins. The meter also has a vane, like a weather vane, that records the direction of the current.

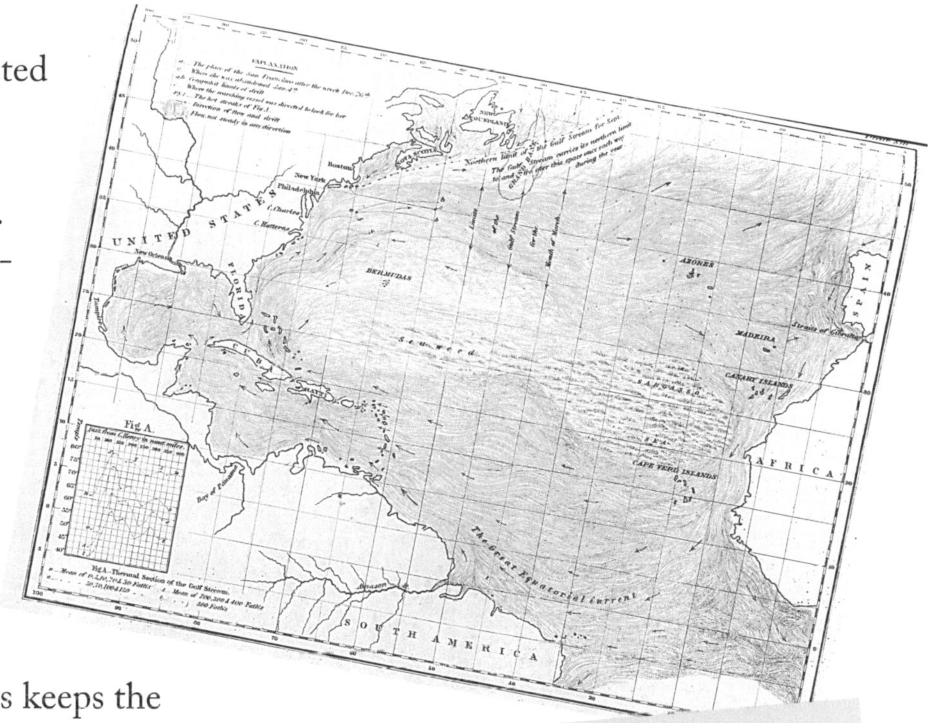

(above)
Matthew Maury used information from captains' logs to make this current map for the 1858 edition of Wind and Current Charts.

(left)
Today oceanographers use drifter information as well as satellite pictures, like this one of currents in the Gulf Stream, to help them make charts.

Benjamin Franklin was a visionary, a person whose imagination reached into the future. Much of today's science is based on the ideas of people like Franklin.

Studying the Gulf Stream from Space

Scientists also use methods to track the Gulf Stream that even Franklin never imagined. In 1992 scientists sent a satellite into space to take pictures of the Gulf Stream—not to replace all the other tools, but to add more information about the path of the Stream. Other satellites show the water temperature of the ocean's surface—red for warmer water, blue for colder water.

When scientists like WHOI oceanographer Phil Richardson look at satellite images, they think of Franklin's charts of the Gulf Stream. About 20 years ago, Phil asked another researcher, Fritz Fuglister, for the best chart of the Stream. Fritz, who had spent many years charting the Stream, said it was thought that the Franklin-Folger chart was still the best. But nobody could find it.

There were later charts, but after reading Franklin's notes about the first chart, Phil thought later copies might not be as good as the first one. He decided to find the first chart and wrote to scientists all over the world. Nobody had the chart. Nobody had even seen it. On a trip to France in 1978, Phil had an idea. Maybe the chart was in the French National Library. Franklin had spent many years in France. Did he hide the chart from the British there? Sure enough, Phil found the very first chart of the Gulf Stream in a folder in the library. It turned out that the second chart was a copy of the first one. Looking at the chart in the French library, Phil was struck again by how good the picture of the Gulf Stream was. Even today, it's still the best "big picture" look at the Gulf Stream.

By looking at Franklin's chart and satellite images and by using new tools, oceanographers can understand the Gulf Stream better than ever before.

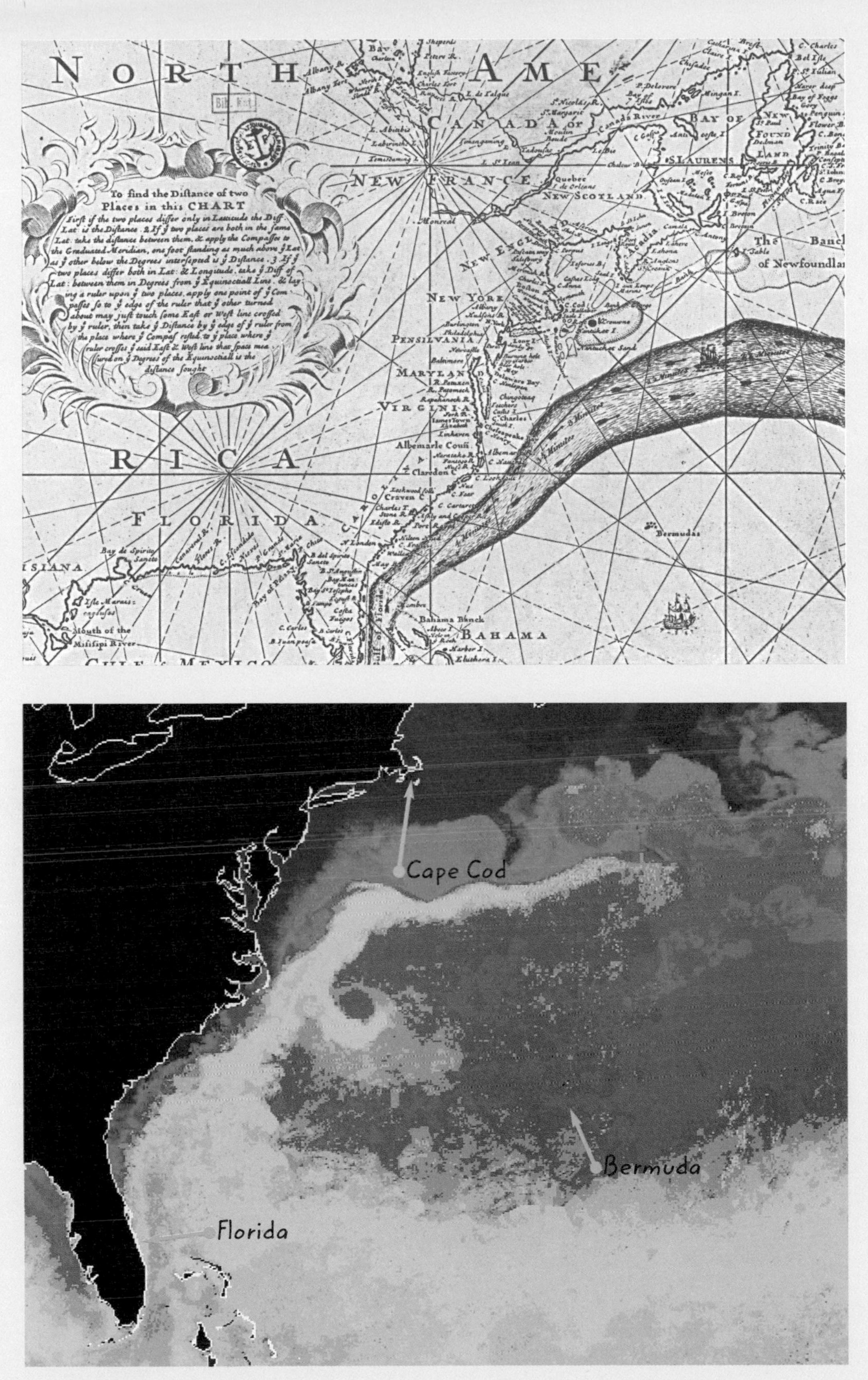

Old and New

It is interesting to compare Benjamin Franklin's 1769–70 chart (top) of the average path of the Gulf Stream with a modern-day satellite image (bottom). The satellite that made this image records the temperature of the ocean surface. The warmer Gulf Stream water shows up as bright orange.

Both images trace the Stream's path from the tip of Florida out into the Atlantic Ocean about as far as Bermuda. (Franklin's chart also shows the Stream beyond Bermuda.) Both images show the Stream leaving the coast near Cape Cod in Massachusetts. And both show the Stream moving over Bermuda in a similar curve.

5 The Wild Whirl of Water

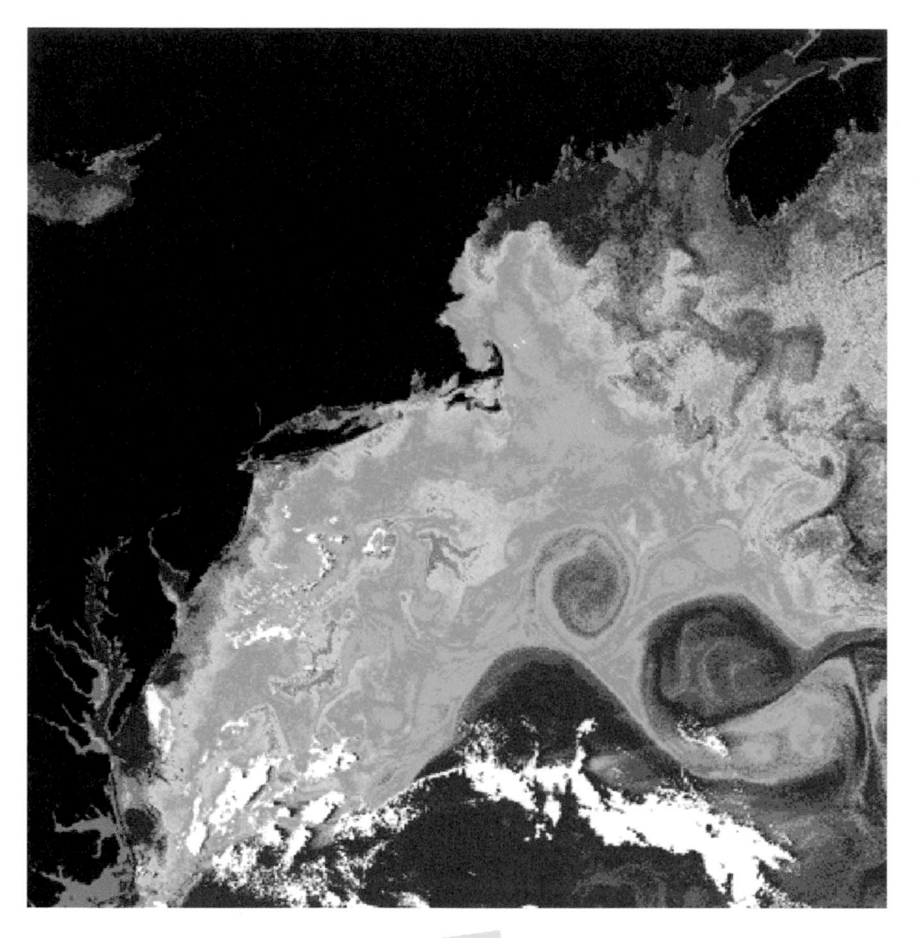

The wild, swirling waters of the Gulf Stream don't always flow in one direction. Sometimes pieces of the Stream break off and spin around on their own.

Although they still haven't uncovered all the Gulf Stream's secrets, scientists now have a good picture of the ocean superhighway. They have learned how fast the Gulf Stream moves and where it goes. They have also learned how the Gulf Stream can make a place warmer. The Gulf Stream acts like a **conveyer belt**, bringing warm water north from the equator.

Here's how it works. Water in the ocean is heated by the sun. The sunlight is strongest at the equator, so water at the equator is very warm. That warm water moves north. As the Gulf Stream's warmer water rushes through the North Atlantic Ocean, the Stream warms the water around it. The Gulf Stream also warms the air over it, just like your hand gets warm if you put it over a cup of hot chocolate. The winds then warm the land near the water. It's because of the Gulf Stream and westerly winds, for example, that Great Britain is much warmer in the winter than Newfoundland, Canada, even though both places are just as far north.

The North Atlantic Gyre

As Prince Albert learned, the Gulf Stream is actually part of a bigger system of currents in the North Atlantic Ocean, called the North Atlantic **Gyre** (pronounced "JIRE"). The North Atlantic Gyre is a big wheel of currents that moves clockwise in the ocean. The Gyre runs along the coast of North America and then turns right toward Europe. Prince Albert helped trace the Gyre's path a hundred years ago. Since then other scientists have studied it and have learned more about the Gyre's direction and speed.

Scientists found that the Gulf Stream moves faster along the coast of Florida than anywhere else. When it's rushing past Florida's coast and through a narrow water passage called the Straits of Florida, the Gulf Stream moves at about 160 kilometers (about 100 miles) a day, or 6.5 kilometers (about 4 miles) per hour. That means that if you were in a ship with the engine turned off and the sails down, you could still move 160 kilometers north in one day just by taking a ride on the Gulf Stream here. The Stream also moves a lot of water past Florida. It carries more than 30,000,000 cubic meters (about 1,000,000,000 cubic feet) of water a second. That's about 400,000 backyard-sized swimming pools full of water each second.

Oceanographers knew that the reason water moves faster by Florida is that the Gyre's center is much closer to Florida than to Africa. Think of the North Atlantic Gyre as a circle in the middle of the ocean. When the current goes past Africa, it has room to spread out, so it moves more slowly. When

The Gulf Stream affects the **climate** in many places. The Gulf Stream makes the water so warm that in parts of Ireland, palm trees grow.

Like **rapids** rushing through a narrow space, the thin red line of the Gulf Stream can be seen rushing through the narrow space between Florida and the Bahamas. But even if the Bahamas weren't there, the Stream would still be narrow along Florida's coast because of where the center of the North Atlantic Gyre is located.

it moves past North America, the same amount of water has to get through a narrower space, so it moves faster. But there was something that puzzled scientists for a long time—why was the center of the Gyre closer to North American than to Africa?

In the late 1940s, oceanographer Henry Stommel figured out the answer while scribbling on a napkin in a coffee shop. What he found was that wind and the earth's shape and rotation all affect the Gyre's shape, and make the center closer to North America than to Africa. Stommel had solved the puzzle of the Gyre.

Following the Stream

The Gulf Stream, however, isn't simple. It is not just a band of moving water. The more scientists study it, the more they realize just how complicated it is. For example, the Gulf Stream doesn't stay in one place. It meanders, or moves sideways. Since the Gulf Stream flows through water, there are no hard banks or edges of land to keep it on one path. It can meander from day to day or from week to week.

Sometimes part of the Stream moves. This is called a meander, and if it loops back on itself, a meander can close and become a ring. Remember Williams, Franklin's grandnephew? He discovered a ring of warm water from the Gulf Stream. Scientists now spend a lot of time studying the Gulf Stream meanders and rings.

One of these scientists is Nelson Hogg. He wants to know why the Stream meanders and why water moves out from the Stream and then comes back.

These satellite images of water temperature show how the Gulf Stream meanders. The Stream shows as dark orange in each image. The image on the left was made on August 18, 1998. The image on the right was made on October 26, 1998. The arrows below show one place where the Stream has meandered during that time.

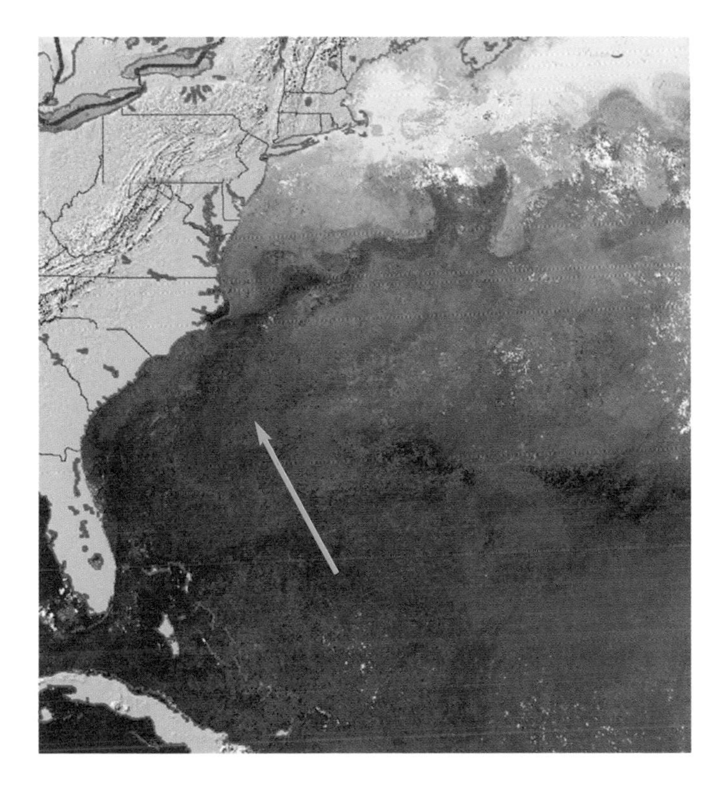

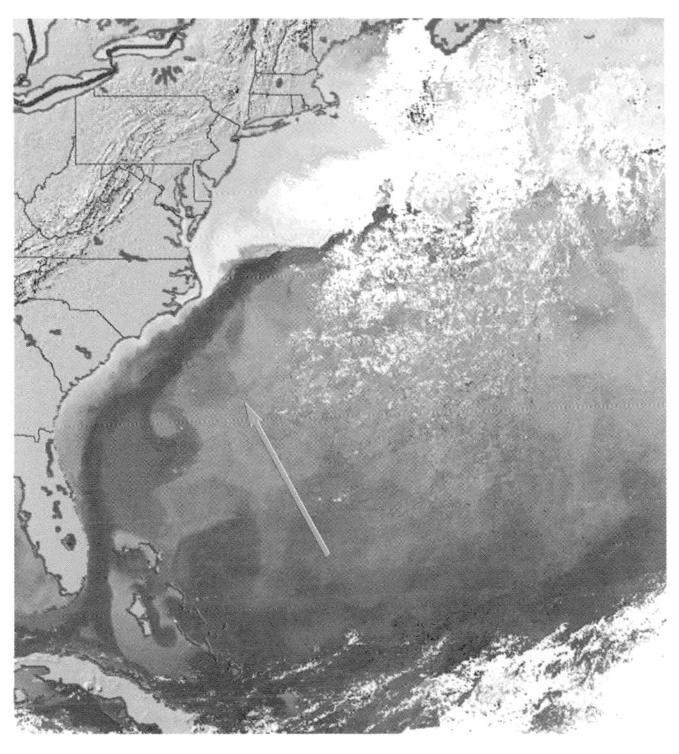

Ring Bob

In 1977 when Phil Richardson observed with satellite measurements that a meander had just broken away as a ring south of the Gulf Stream, he decided to go see for himself. He and some of his fellow oceanographers set sail on the WHOI research vessel *Knorr*. Plotting its course from satellite data, Richardson found a brand-new ring that had formed from the meander. Rings are large—they can be from 100 to 300 kilometers (about 60 to 185 miles) in diameter. Rings are made of Gulf Stream water. Some rings have cold water from north of the Stream in the middle. Others have warm water from the south in the middle. As soon as they got near it, Phil's crew could actually smell the water inside the ring. Phil said it smelled like "the seashore on a summer day." The ring was shaped like a big blue donut, about 250 kilometers (150 miles) in diameter with brown water in the middle.

Phil named this ring Bob, after a fellow oceanographer. He plotted Ring Bob's course by satellite buoy and went back to visit it during the next few months to get a picture of a ring from its start to its finish. But Bob wasn't the only ring in the ocean. Below you can see the paths of Ring Bob and seven neighboring rings, along with each ring's beginning and ending dates. Some rings last for six months, while others may last up to one or two years, or even longer.

1 Dave—April 10, 1977—September 1977
2 Charlie—April 12, 1977—November 21, 1977
3 Bob—April 14, 1977—September 17, 1977
4 Allen—December 4, 1976—April 1, 1977
5 Joyce—June 17, 1977—July 19, 1977
6 Arthur—December 14, 1976—August 10, 1977
7 Ring R—September 27, 1977—October 17, 1977
8 Ring Q—November 17, 1977—December 1977

He thinks the answer may lie in the different water temperatures in and around the Gulf Stream. Because warm water moves on top of cold water, it could be that the different temperatures, along with winds, cause meanders. Some meanders break off and turn into rings, trapping water inside. These rings sometimes move away from the Stream.

Rings also affect people. Rings are strong enough to tear lobster traps away from the moorings that attach them to the seafloor. Before we knew about rings, fishers in the United States used to blame their lost lobster traps on foreign fishers. They thought other people had stolen their traps, when it was really rings of water that had pulled them away. Ships can also use rings to get around faster, the same way ships have used the Gulf Stream to speed up travel for centuries.

Sailors who know about a ring can move into it and ride it like a high-speed train—getting where they want to go faster. Some yacht racers use the rings when they compete. They go to "ring briefings" before races to find out the latest on where rings are and where they're going.

Oceanographers aren't finished studying the Gulf Stream. Phil Richardson, Nelson Hogg, and others are studying the Stream's meanders and rings. Amy Bower is working to find out how the Deep Western Boundary Current and the Gulf Steam cross each other and how both affect our climate. There is still a lot scientists don't know about the Gulf Stream. But by using new tools, old wisdom, and the inventiveness of Benjamin Franklin, they will keep uncovering the mysteries of the ocean highway.

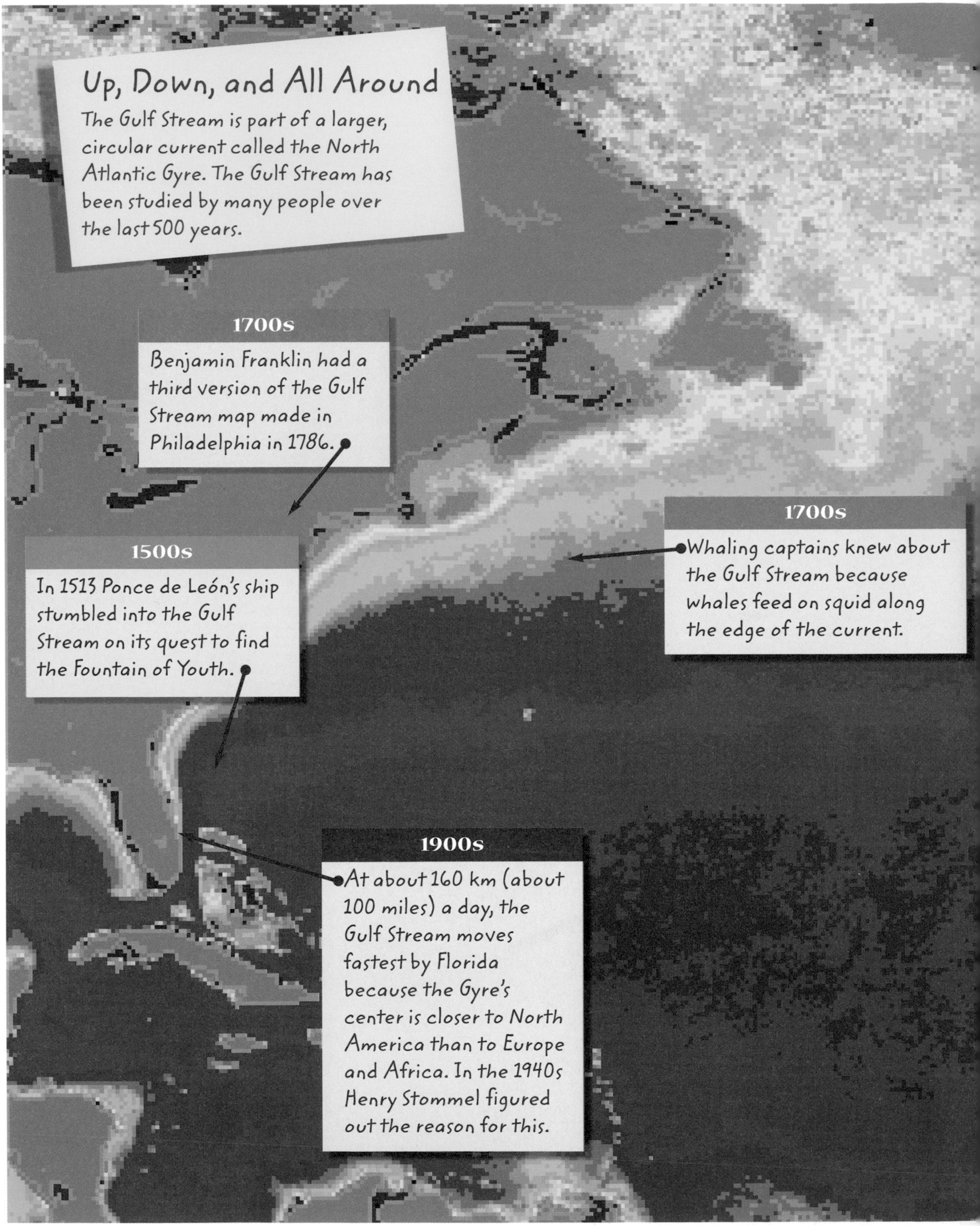

Up, Down, and All Around

The Gulf Stream is part of a larger, circular current called the North Atlantic Gyre. The Gulf Stream has been studied by many people over the last 500 years.

1700s

Benjamin Franklin had a third version of the Gulf Stream map made in Philadelphia in 1786.

1500s

In 1513 Ponce de León's ship stumbled into the Gulf Stream on its quest to find the Fountain of Youth.

1700s

Whaling captains knew about the Gulf Stream because whales feed on squid along the edge of the current.

1900s

At about 160 km (about 100 miles) a day, the Gulf Stream moves fastest by Florida because the Gyre's center is closer to North America than to Europe and Africa. In the 1940s Henry Stommel figured out the reason for this.

1800s

Using messages inside bottles, Prince Albert learned that the Gulf Stream splits past the banks of Canada. Scientists today use drifters, floats, and buoys.

1700s

Benjamin Franklin and his cousin Timothy Folger created the first chart of the Gulf Stream in London in 1769. But British packet captains wouldn't use it.

1900s

Phil Richardson found the Franklin-Folger Gulf Stream chart in the French National Library in Paris in 1978.

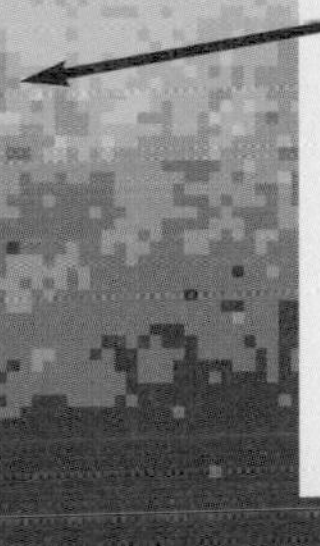

1700s

The Gulf Stream slowed British packets on their way to the Northern Colonies. Captains didn't listen to whalers' advice to avoid the Gulf Stream.

Glossary

anchor [ANG-kor] A heavy object attached to a boat or ship that is thrown overboard to keep the ship in place. Franklin's sea anchor, with a parachute attached, slows down a ship.

buoys [BOO-eez] Floats used to warn ships of a reef, bar, or coast. Also used in oceanography to study currents.

chart A map that shows coastlines, currents, the depth of the water, weather patterns, and other information useful for ocean navigation.

climate The conditions typical for an area, including its temperature, the amount of rainfall and snowfall, and wind.

colonies The thirteen British colonies that fought for independence and became the original United States of America. These colonies were Connecticut, Delaware, Georgia, Maryland, Massachusetts, New Hampshire, New Jersey, New York, North Carolina, Pennsylvania, Rhode Island, South Carolina, and Virginia.

conveyer belt A long belt that is constantly moving. It is often used in factories to move things from one place to another.

current A mass of liquid, such as water, that is in motion.

data [DAY-tuh] Information, often information that will be analyzed or entered into a computer.

eddy A circular flow of water often on the side or edge of a main current.

equator [ee-KWAY-tor] The imaginary line that circles Earth halfway between the North Pole and the South Pole. It is very hot at the equator because the sun shines directly on the equator all year round. Therefore, the air and water at the equator is warmer than the air and water at the poles.

floats Objects designed to ride on the surface of the water.

gyre [JIRE] A moving ring or circle.

latitude [LAT-i-tood] The distance on Earth's surface north or south of the equator. It is measured in degrees. One degree of latitude is about 69 miles on land, or 60 nautical miles.

longitude [LONJ-i-tood] The distance east or west on Earth's surface measured from the Prime Meridian in Greenwich, England.

oceanographer A scientist who studies the ocean.

packets Ships that travel on a regular route carrying passengers, freight, or mail. The ships that carried mail from England to the American colonies were called packets.

rapids A part of a river that moves extremely quickly.

rings Wheels of water that break from a main current and spin in a circular motion.

rivalry [RY-val-ree] Competition.

satellite An object that orbits Earth and relays information back. A satellite can take pictures of weather patterns, ocean currents, and other planets. Communication satellites can transmit TV, radio, and telephone signals.

statesman A person who is a leader in government and politics, especially as a representative abroad, such as an ambassador.

superintendent Someone who is in charge of something. Alexander Bache was the superintendent of the U.S. Coast Survey in charge of the study of the coast of the United States.

thermometer [ther-MOM-i-ter] A tool used for measuring temperature.

transmitters Tools that send information. A sound transmitter sends sound.

Further Reading

Fleisher, Paul. *Our Oceans: Experiments and Activities in Marine Science.* Brookfield, CT: Millbrook Press, 1995.

Fritz, Jean. *What's the Big Idea, Ben Franklin?* New York: Putnam, 1996.

Kiraske, Robert. Illustrated by Brian Floca. *The Voyager's Stone: The Adventures of a Message-Carrying Bottle Adrift on the Ocean Sea.* New York: Orchard Books, 1995.

Lambert, David. *The Kingfisher Young People's Book of Oceans.* New York: Kingfisher Books, 1997.

Simon, Seymour. *How to Be an Ocean Scientist in Your Own Home.* New York: Lippincott, 1988.

Waterlow, Julia. *The Atlantic Ocean.* (Seas and Ocean Series) Austin, TX: Raintree Steck-Vaughn, 1997.

Index

Alaminos, Anton de 4
Albert, Prince of Monaco 24–25, 27, 29, 37, 43

Bachc, Alexander 17–18, 19, 23, 29
Bache, Benjamin Franklin 14
Bache, Lieutenant George 18
Bower, Amy 30–31, 41
British ships 8, 9, 13, 43
buoys 28, 29, 43

Carson, Rachel 7
Cavendish thermometer 14, 19
climate 36–37
CTD 26
current meters 32, 33
currents 6–7, 11–13, 17–23, 29–30, 37–38, 41

Deep Water Western Boundary Current 29–30, 41
derelicts and derelict charts 22, 23
drifter buoys 28, 29, 33, 43

eddy 7, 17
equator, the 16

floats 29–31, 43
Folger, Timothy 11–13, 19
Franklin, Benjamin 8–9, 10–17, 27–28, 33, 34–35, 41, 42, 43
Franklin, Temple 14
Franklin-Folger chart 12–13, 19, 34, 35, 42–43
French National Library 34, 43
Fuglister, Fritz 34

Global Lagrangian Drifter 28
Gulf Stream
  discovered 4–6
  satellite pictures of 6, 33, 35, 36, 38, 39, 40, 42–43
  Benjamin Franklin studies 8–9, 10, 11–13, 14–17, 27, 28, 33–35
  currents in 6–7, 11–13, 18, 22–25, 29–30, 37–38
  Franklin's charts of 12–13, 14–16, 19, 34, 35, 42–43
  temperature in 14, 18, 19, 24, 26–28, 36–37, 41
  Bache and Maury study 17–23, 27 33
  Prince Albert studies 24–25
  scientists study 26–35, 37–41
  speed of 37–38, 42

Hogg, Nelson 39, 41

Knorr (WHOI research vessel) 40

latitude and longitude 16
logbooks from Navy ships 19

mail system 8, 9, 11–13, 43
"Maritime Observations" 16
Maury, Lieutenant Matthew 17, 18–19, 20–21, 22–23, 27, 33
meanders 39–41
meridians 16
mines, explosive 25

National Academy of Sciences 17
Navy. *See United States Navy*
Negretti and Zambra thermometer 24
North Atlantic Gyre 37–38, 42

packets (ships) 8, 9, 13, 43
parallels 16
Ponce de León, Juan 4, 42

RAFOS floats 30–31
Revolutionary War 13, 14
Richardson, Phil 34, 40, 41, 43
rings 39–41
Ring Bob 40

salinity (saltiness) 26, 27
San Francisco (ship) 22
sea anchor 10
ships. *See British ships; mail system; packets; United States Navy; whaling ships*
Six, James, and Six thermometer 19
Stommel, Henry 29, 37–38, 42
Swallow, John 29
Swallow float 29

temperature. *See Gulf Stream*
thermistor 27
thermometers 28
  Cavendish 14, 19
  Six 19, 24
  Negretti and Zambra 24
  XBT 27

United States Coast Survey 17
United States Navy
  Depot of Charts and
    Instruments 18–19

whaling ships and captains 11–12, 19, 20, 33, 42
Williams, Jonathan 16-17, 39
Wind and Current Charts 19, 33
Woods Hole Oceanographic Institution (WHOI) 29, 30, 34, 40

XBT thermometer 27

Acknowledgments

The author would like to thank Amy Bower, Ellen Cohen, Roy Goodman, Nelson Hogg, Phil Richardson, Nancy Sandberg, and Jonathan Weiner.

Photographs courtesy of:

Allen, Jeff/Nantucket Historical Association: 11 top and bottom; American Philosophical Society: front cover inset, 10 top, 17, 34; *Benjamin Franklin* by Francois Denis Nee/Philadelphia Museum of Art: 13; Bord Failte-Irish Tourist Board: 37; Coastal Zone Scanner Project, NASA Goddard Space Flight Center: 6 top, 36, 42, 43; Corbett, T./Woods Hole Oceanographic Institution: 32; Cornillon, Peter/University of Rhode Island: 35 bottom, 38; Day, Richard and Susan/*Animals Animals:* 3 top; Dean, Jerry/Woods Hole Oceanographic Institution: 26; Fisichella, David/Woods Hole Oceanographic Institution: 31; GOOS Center at NOAA's Atlantic Oceanographic and Meteorological Laboratory: 28 top; *Grands Voyages,* Theodor de Bry, Frankfurt, 1594/Tozzer Library, Harvard University: 5; Greenberg, Phyllis/*Animals Animals,* 2–3 bottom; Huber, F./*Animals Animals:* 2 top; Knight, Chris/The New Film Company, Inc.: 41; "Maritime Observations" by Benjamin Franklin from the *Transactions of the American Philosophical Society,* Vol. 2, 1786/Widener Library, Harvard University: 10 bottom, 15; Mary Evans Picture Library, London: 25; Wind and Current Charts by M. F. Maury from *Maury's Sailing Directions,* 1958/Widener Library, Harvard University: 20, 21, 33 top; National Portrait Gallery, Smithsonian Institution: 18 top; *Natural History Magazine,* Harlan, Iowa, Vol. 94, No. 6, June 1985: 23; Naval Historical Foundation: 22; *New York Harbour* by Thomas Birch/Museum of Fine Arts, Boston: 8; Ocean Remote Sensing Group, Johns Hopkins University Applied Physics Laboratory: 1 (title page), 33 bottom, 39 left and right; Popperfoto, Northhampton, England: 24 top; National Archives/Salem Museum: 18 bottom; Richardson, Phil/Bibliothèque Nationale de France: 12, 35 top; Rosensteil School of Marine and Atmospheric Science, University of Miami: front cover; Watt, James/*Animals Animals*: 7; Woods Hole Oceanographic Institution: 27, 29, 30; Zuraw, Thomas/*Animals Animals*: 6 bottom.

Illustrations on pages 4, 9, 16, and 40 are by David Stevenson. Illustrations on pages 14, 19, 24 bottom, 27, 28, and 30 are by Katherine Brown-Wing.